SOUND ORCHESTRA

ENSEMBLE DEVELOPMENT
STRING or FULL ORCHESTRA

Warm-Up Exercises and Chorales to Improve Blend, Balance, Intonation, Phrasing, and Articulation

FOR INTERMEDIATE through ADVANCED ENSEMBLES

Bob **PHILLIPS** | Peter **BOONSHAFT** | Chris **BERNOTAS** | Jim **PALMER** | David **POPE**

MW00975255

)LA

Welcome to *Sound Orchestra*! It is our hope you will find this book to be a valuable resource in helping you grow in your understanding and abilities as an ensemble musician. This method is designed to be used by a string orchestra, a full orchestra, or any combination of strings, winds, percussion, or keyboard.

The book is organized by key, and an assortment of exercises and chorales are presented in a variety of difficulty levels. Where possible, several exercises in the same category are provided to create variety while accomplishing the goals of that specific type of exercise. You will notice that many exercises and chorales are clearly marked with dynamics, articulations, and style markings for you to practice those aspects of performance. Other exercises are intentionally left unmarked for you or your teacher to determine how best to use them in facilitating the goals and addressing the needs of the ensemble.

Whether you are progressing through exercises to better your technical facility, challenging your musicianship with beautiful chorales, or playing arrangements of excerpts from orchestral repertoire, we are confident you will be excited, motivated, and inspired by using *Sound Orchestra*.

ATLANTA INTERNATIONAL SCHOOL ORCHESTRA

alfred.com

Copyright © 2022 by Alfred Music
All rights reserved. Printed in USA.

ISBN-10: 1-4706-4840-7
ISBN-13: 978-1-4706-4840-4

Instrument photos courtesy of Yamaha Corporation of America Band & Orchestral Division

Concert G Major

1 TUNING

Full Orchestra: Play 3 times—strings tacet 2nd time.
String Orchestra: Perform as written.

2 PASSING THE TONIC

3 PASSING THE TONIC

4 CONCERT G MAJOR SCALE AND ARPEGGIO

5 CHROMATIC SCALE

6 SCALE PATTERN

7 BALANCE AND INTONATION: PERFECT INTERVALS

8 BALANCE AND INTONATION: DIATONIC HARMONY

9 BALANCE AND INTONATION: FAMILY BALANCE

10 BALANCE AND INTONATION: FAMILY BALANCE

11 BALANCE AND INTONATION: LAYERED TUNING

12 BALANCE AND INTONATION: SHIFTING CHORD QUALITIES

13 DYNAMICS

14 ARTICULATION

15 RHYTHMIC SUBDIVISION

16 PHRASING

17 PHRASING

18 CONCERT G MAJOR SCALE & CHORALE

Chris M. Bernotas (ASCAP)

19 CHORALE: BWV 399

Johann Sebastian Bach (1685–1750)
Arranged by Chris M. Bernotas (ASCAP)

20 CHORALE

Chris M. Bernotas (ASCAP)

21 **ORCHESTRAL REPERTOIRE: Symphony No. 100**

Franz Joseph Haydn (1732–1809)
Arranged by Bob Phillips (ASCAP)

22 **ORCHESTRAL REPERTOIRE: March from *The Nutcracker***

Piotr Ilyich Tchaikovsky (1840–1893)
Arranged by Bob Phillips (ASCAP)

23 **ORCHESTRAL REPERTOIRE: Trepak from *The Nutcracker***

Piotr Ilyich Tchaikovsky (1840–1893)
Arranged by Bob Phillips (ASCAP)

Concert E Minor

24 PASSING THE TONIC

25 PASSING THE TONIC

26 CONCERT E MINOR SCALE AND ARPEGGIO

27 SCALE PATTERN

28 BALANCE AND INTONATION: PERFECT INTERVALS

29 BALANCE AND INTONATION: DIATONIC HARMONY

30 BALANCE AND INTONATION: FAMILY BALANCE

31 BALANCE AND INTONATION: FAMILY BALANCE

32 BALANCE AND INTONATION: LAYERED TUNING

33 DYNAMICS

34 ARTICULATION

35 RHYTHMIC SUBDIVISION

36 PHRASING

8

37 CONCERT E MINOR SCALE & CHORALE

Chris M. Bernotas (ASCAP)

38 CHORALE: BWV 4

Johann Sebastian Bach (1685–1750)
Arranged by Bob Phillips (ASCAP)

39 CHORALE

Chris M. Bernotas (ASCAP)

40 ORCHESTRAL REPERTOIRE: Symphony No. 5

Piotr Ilyich Tchaikovsky (1840–1893)
Arranged by Bob Phillips (ASCAP)

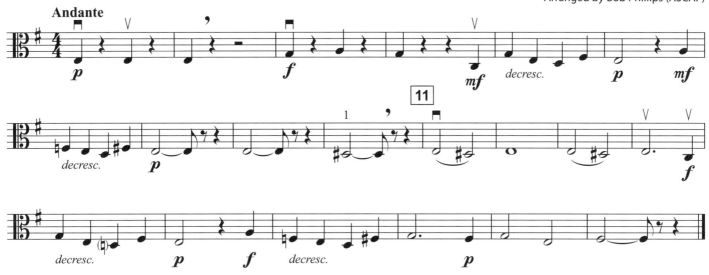

41 ORCHESTRAL REPERTOIRE: The Moldau

Bedrich Smetana (1824–1884)
Arranged by Bob Phillips (ASCAP)

42 ORCHESTRAL REPERTOIRE: Symphony No. 9

Antonín Dvořák (1841–1904)
Arranged by Bob Phillips (ASCAP)

Concert D Major

43 **PASSING THE TONIC**

44 **PASSING THE TONIC**

45 **CONCERT D MAJOR SCALE AND ARPEGGIO**

46 **CHROMATIC SCALE**

47 **SCALE PATTERN**

48 **BALANCE AND INTONATION: PERFECT INTERVALS**

49 **BALANCE AND INTONATION: DIATONIC HARMONY**

50 **BALANCE AND INTONATION: FAMILY BALANCE**

51 BALANCE AND INTONATION: FAMILY BALANCE

For this exercise, and others like it, div. will only be marked at the first instance. Other measures with multiple notes should also be divisi.

52 BALANCE AND INTONATION: LAYERED TUNING

53 BALANCE AND INTONATION: SHIFTING CHORD QUALITIES

54 DYNAMICS

55 ARTICULATION

56 ARTICULATION

57 RHYTHMIC SUBDIVISION

58 PHRASING

59 CONCERT D MAJOR SCALE & CHORALE

Chris M. Bernotas (ASCAP)

60 CHORALE: BWV 303

Johann Sebastian Bach (1685–1750)
Arranged by Bob Phillips (ASCAP)

61 CHORALE

Chris M. Bernotas (ASCAP)

62 **ORCHESTRAL REPERTOIRE: Symphony No. 6**

Piotr Ilyich Tchaikovsky (1840–1893)
Arranged by Bob Phillips (ASCAP)

63 **ORCHESTRAL REPERTOIRE: Symphony No. 2**

Jean Sibelius (1865–1957)
Arranged by Bob Phillips (ASCAP)

64 **ORCHESTRAL REPERTOIRE: Symphony No. 9**

Ludwig van Beethoven (1770–1827)
Arranged by Bob Phillips (ASCAP)

Concert B Minor

65 PASSING THE TONIC

66 PASSING THE TONIC

67 CONCERT B MINOR SCALE AND ARPEGGIO

68 SCALE PATTERN

69 BALANCE AND INTONATION: PERFECT INTERVALS

70 BALANCE AND INTONATION: DIATONIC HARMONY

71 BALANCE AND INTONATION: FAMILY BALANCE

72 BALANCE AND INTONATION: FAMILY BALANCE

15

73 BALANCE AND INTONATION: LAYERED TUNING

74 DYNAMICS

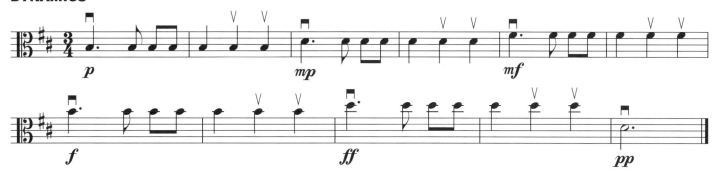

75 ARTICULATION

76 ARTICULATION

77 RHYTHMIC SUBDIVISION

78 PHRASING

16

79 CONCERT B MINOR SCALE & CHORALE

Chris M. Bernotas (ASCAP)

80 CHORALE: BWV 62

Johann Sebastian Bach (1685–1750)
Arranged by Bob Phillips (ASCAP)

81 CHORALE

Chris M. Bernotas (ASCAP)

With grace

82 **ORCHESTRAL REPERTOIRE: Symphony No. 2**

Alexander Borodin (1833–1887)
Arranged by Bob Phillips (ASCAP)

83 **ORCHESTRAL REPERTOIRE: Aase's Death from _Peer Gynt Suite No. 1_**

Edvard Grieg (1843–1907)
Arranged by Bob Phillips (ASCAP)

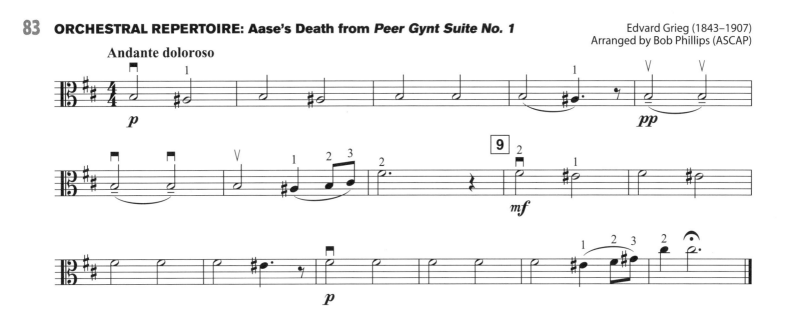

84 **ORCHESTRAL REPERTOIRE: Symphony No. 8**

Franz Schubert (1797–1828)
Arranged by Bob Phillips (ASCAP)

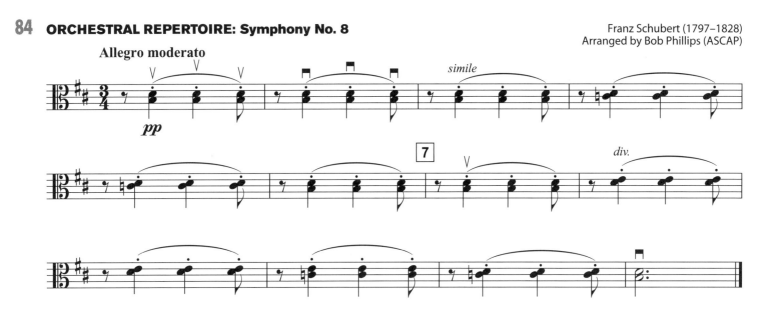

Concert C Major

85 PASSING THE TONIC

86 PASSING THE TONIC

87 CONCERT C MAJOR SCALE AND ARPEGGIO

88 CHROMATIC SCALE

89 SCALE PATTERN

90 BALANCE AND INTONATION: PERFECT INTERVALS

91 BALANCE AND INTONATION: DIATONIC HARMONY

92 BALANCE AND INTONATION: FAMILY BALANCE

93 BALANCE AND INTONATION: FAMILY BALANCE

94 BALANCE AND INTONATION: LAYERED TUNING

95 BALANCE AND INTONATION: SHIFTING CHORD QUALITIES

96 DYNAMICS

97 ARTICULATION

98 RHYTHMIC SUBDIVISION

99 PHRASING

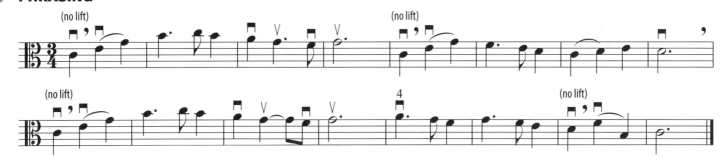

100 CONCERT C MAJOR SCALE & CHORALE

Chris M. Bernotas (ASCAP)

101 CHORALE: BWV 248

Johann Sebastian Bach (1685–1750)
Arranged by Bob Phillips (ASCAP)

102 CHORALE

Chris M. Bernotas (ASCAP)

103 ORCHESTRAL REPERTOIRE: Symphony No. 5

Ludwig van Beethoven (1770–1827)
Arranged by Bob Phillips (ASCAP)

104 ORCHESTRAL REPERTOIRE: Die Meistersinger

Richard Wagner (1813–1883)
Arranged by Bob Phillips (ASCAP)

105 ORCHESTRAL REPERTOIRE: Symphony No. 1

Johannes Brahms (1833–1897)
Arranged by Bob Phillips (ASCAP)

Concert A Minor

106 **PASSING THE TONIC**

107 **PASSING THE TONIC**

108 **CONCERT A MINOR SCALE AND ARPEGGIO**

109 **SCALE PATTERN**

110 **BALANCE AND INTONATION: PERFECT INTERVALS**

111 **BALANCE AND INTONATION: DIATONIC HARMONY**

112 **BALANCE AND INTONATION: FAMILY BALANCE**

113 **BALANCE AND INTONATION: FAMILY BALANCE**

23

114 BALANCE AND INTONATION: LAYERD TUNING

115 DYNAMICS

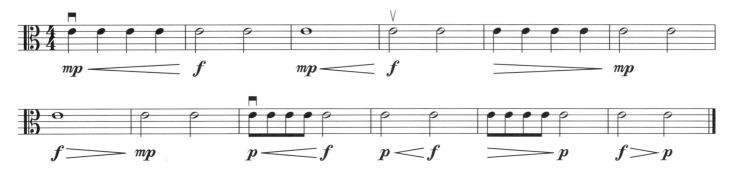

116 ARTICULATION

117 RHYTHMIC SUBDIVISION

118 PHRASING

119 CONCERT A MINOR SCALE & CHORALE

Chris M. Bernotas (ASCAP)

120 CHORALE: BWV 330

Johann Sebastian Bach (1685–1750)
Arranged by Bob Phillips (ASCAP)

121 CHORALE

Chris M. Bernotas (ASCAP)

122 ORCHESTRAL REPERTOIRE: Symphony No. 7

Ludwig van Beethoven (1770–1827)
Arranged by Bob Phillips (ASCAP)

123 ORCHESTRAL REPERTOIRE: Symphony No. 3

Felix Mendelssohn (1809–1847)
Arranged by Bob Phillips (ASCAP)

124 ORCHESTRAL REPERTOIRE: Symphony No. 4

Felix Mendelssohn (1804–1847)
Arranged by Bob Phillips (ASCAP)

Concert F Major

125 **PASSING THE TONIC**

126 **PASSING THE TONIC**

127 **CONCERT F MAJOR SCALE AND ARPEGGIO**

128 **CHROMATIC SCALE**

129 **SCALE PATTERN**

130 **BALANCE AND INTONATION: PERFECT INTERVALS**

131 **BALANCE AND INTONATION: DIATONIC HARMONY**

132 **BALANCE AND INTONATION: FAMILY BALANCE**

133 BALANCE AND INTONATION: FAMILY BALANCE

134 BALANCE AND INTONATION: LAYERED TUNING

135 BALANCE AND INTONATION: SHIFTING CHORD QUALITIES

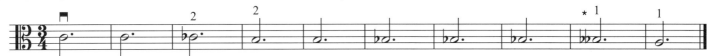

136 DYNAMICS

137 ARTICULATION

138 RHYTHMIC SUBDIVISION

139 PHRASING

140 PHRASING

* A double flat (♭♭) lowers the pitch of a note two *half steps* or one *whole step*.

141 **CONCERT F MAJOR SCALE & CHORALE**
Chris M. Bernotas (ASCAP)

142 **CHORALE: BWV 180**
Johann Sebastian Bach (1685–1750)
Arranged by Bob Phillips (ASCAP)

143 **CHORALE**
Chris M. Bernotas (ASCAP)

144 **ORCHESTRAL REPERTOIRE: Symphony No. 6**

Ludwig van Beethoven (1770–1827)
Arranged by Bob Phillips (ASCAP)

Allegro ma non troppo

145 **ORCHESTRAL REPERTOIRE: Ruslan and Ludmilla**

Mikhail Glinka (1804–1857)
Arranged by Bob Phillips (ASCAP)

Presto

146 **ORCHESTRAL REPERTOIRE: Capriccio Espagnol**

Nikolai Rimsky-Korsakov (1844–1908)
Arranged by Bob Phillips (ASCAP)

Andante con moto

30

Concert D Minor

147 PASSING THE TONIC

148 PASSING THE TONIC

149 CONCERT D MINOR SCALE AND ARPEGGIO

150 SCALE PATTERN

151 BALANCE AND INTONATION: PERFECT INTERVALS

152 BALANCE AND INTONATION: DIATONIC HARMONY

153 BALANCE AND INTONATION: FAMILY BALANCE

154 BALANCE AND INTONATION: FAMILY BALANCE

155 BALANCE AND INTONATION: LAYERED TUNING

156 DYNAMICS

157 ARTICULATION

158 RHYTHMIC SUBDIVISION

159 PHRASING

32

160 CONCERT D MINOR SCALE & CHORALE

Chris M. Bernotas (ASCAP)

161 CHORALE: BWV 310

Johann Sebastian Bach (1685–1750)
Arranged by Bob Phillips (ASCAP)

162 CHORALE

Chris M. Bernotas (ASCAP)

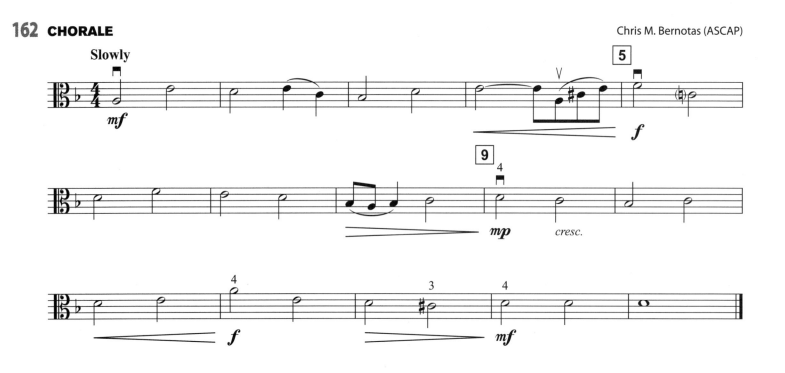

163 ORCHESTRAL REPERTOIRE: **Symphony No. 1**

Gustav Mahler (1860–1911)
Arranged by Bob Phillips (ASCAP)

Feierlich und gemessen, obne zu schieppen

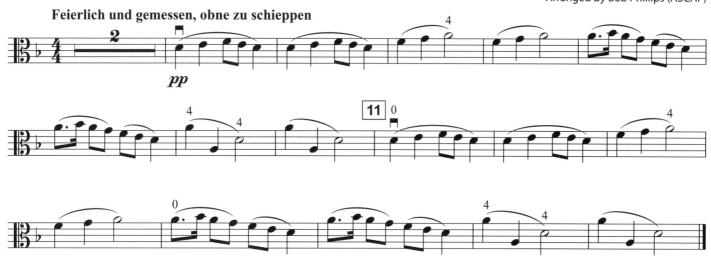

164 ORCHESTRAL REPERTOIRE: **Symphony No. 3**

Gustav Mahler (1860–1911)
Arranged by Bob Phillips (ASCAP)

Kräfig, Entaschleden

165 ORCHESTRAL REPERTOIRE: **Symphony in D minor**

César Franck (1822–1890)
Arranged by Bob Phillips (ASCAP)

Allegro non troppo

Concert B♭ Major

166 PASSING THE TONIC

167 CONCERT B♭ MAJOR SCALE AND ARPEGGIO

168 CHROMATIC SCALE

169 SCALE PATTERN

170 BALANCE AND INTONATION: PERFECT INTERVALS

171 BALANCE AND INTONATION: DIATONIC HARMONY

172 BALANCE AND INTONATION: LAYERED TUNING

173 BALANCE AND INTONATION: SHIFTING CHORD QUALITIES

174 DYNAMICS

175 ARTICULATION

176 PHRASING AND ARTICULATION

177 CONCERT B♭ MAJOR SCALE & CHORALE

Chris M. Bernotas (ASCAP)

178 CHORALE: BWV 307

Johann Sebastian Bach (1685–1750)
Arranged by Bob Phillips (ASCAP)

179 CHORALE

Chris M. Bernotas (ASCAP)

180 ORCHESTRAL REPERTOIRE: Marche Slav

Piotr Ilyich Tchaikovsky (1840–1893)
Arranged by Jim Palmer (ASCAP)

Concert G Minor

181 **PASSING THE TONIC**

182 **CONCERT G MINOR SCALE AND ARPEGGIO**

183 **SCALE PATTERN**

184 **BALANCE AND INTONATION: DIATONIC HARMONY**

185 **BALANCE AND INTONATION: FAMILY BALANCE**

186 **BALANCE AND INTONATION: LAYERED TUNING**

187 **DYNAMICS**

188 ARTICULATION

189 PHRASING AND ARTICULATION

190 CONCERT G MINOR SCALE & CHORALE

Chris M. Bernotas (ASCAP)

191 CHORALE: BWV 274

Johann Sebastian Bach (1685–1750)
Arranged by Bob Phillips (ASCAP)

192 CHORALE

Chris M. Bernotas (ASCAP)

193 ORCHESTRAL REPERTOIRE: Symphony No. 8

Antonín Dvořák (1841–1904)
Arranged by Jim Palmer (ASCAP)

Concert E♭ Major

194 PASSING THE TONIC

195 CONCERT E♭ MAJOR SCALE AND ARPEGGIO

196 CHROMATIC SCALE

197 SCALE PATTERN

198 BALANCE AND INTONATION: PERFECT INTERVALS

199 BALANCE AND INTONATION: DIATONIC HARMONY

200 BALANCE AND INTONATION: LAYERED TUNING

201 BALANCE AND INTONATION: SHIFTING CHORD QUALITIES

202 DYNAMICS

203 ARTICULATION

204 PHRASING AND ARTICULATION

205 CONCERT E♭ MAJOR SCALE & CHORALE — Chris M. Bernotas (ASCAP)

206 CHORALE: BWV 400 — Johann Sebastian Bach (1685–1750) / Arranged by Bob Phillips (ASCAP)

207 CHORALE — Chris M. Bernotas (ASCAP)

208 ORCHESTRAL REPERTOIRE: Jupiter from *The Planets* — Gustav Holst (1874–1934) / Arranged by Jim Palmer (ASCAP)

Concert C Minor

209 **PASSING THE TONIC**

210 **CONCERT C MINOR SCALE AND ARPEGGIO**

211 **SCALE PATTERN**

212 **BALANCE AND INTONATION: PERFECT INTERVALS**

213 **BALANCE AND INTONATION: DIATONIC HARMONY**

214 **BALANCE AND INTONATION: FAMILY BALANCE**

215 **BALANCE AND INTONATION: LAYERED TUNING**

216 **DYNAMICS**

217 ARTICULATION

218 PHRASING AND ARTICULATION

219 CONCERT C MINOR SCALE & CHORALE

Chris M. Bernotas (ASCAP)

220 CHORALE: Lob sei Gott from BWV 36

Johann Sebastian Bach (1685–1750)
Arranged by Bob Phillips (ASCAP)

221 CHORALE

Chris M. Bernotas (ASCAP)

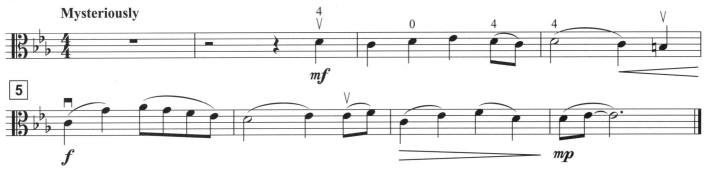

222 ORCHESTRAL REPERTOIRE: Komm, Süsser Tod

Johann Sebastian Bach (1685–1750)
Arranged by Jim Palmer (ASCAP)

42

Concert A Major

223 PASSING THE TONIC

224 CONCERT A MAJOR SCALE AND ARPEGGIO

225 CHROMATIC SCALE

226 SCALE PATTERN

227 BALANCE AND INTONATION: PERFECT INTERVALS

228 BALANCE AND INTONATION: DIATONIC HARMONY

229 BALANCE AND INTONATION: LAYERED TUNING

230 DYNAMICS

231 ARTICULATION

232 PHRASING AND ARTICULATION

233 CONCERT A MAJOR SCALE & CHORALE

Chris M. Bernotas (ASCAP)

A

B

234 CHORALE: BWV 104

Johann Sebastian Bach (1685–1750)
Arranged by Bob Phillips (ASCAP)

235 CHORALE

Chris M. Bernotas (ASCAP)

236 ORCHESTRAL REPERTOIRE: Pastorale from *L'Arlesienne Suite No. 2*

Georges Bizet (1838–1875)
Arranged by Jim Palmer (ASCAP)

Andante sostenuto assai

44

Concert F# Minor

237 PASSING THE TONIC

238 CONCERT F# MINOR SCALE AND ARPEGGIO

239 SCALE PATTERN

240 BALANCE AND INTONATION: PERFECT INTERVALS

241 BALANCE AND INTONATION: DIATONIC HARMONY

242 BALANCE AND INTONATION: FAMILY BALANCE

243 BALANCE AND INTONATION: LAYERED TUNING

244 DYNAMICS

245 ARTICULATION

246 PHRASING AND ARTICULATION

247 CONCERT F♯ MINOR SCALE & CHORALE

Chris M. Bernotas (ASCAP)

A

B

248 CHORALE: BWV 666

Johann Sebastian Bach (1685–1750)
Arranged by Bob Phillips (ASCAP)

249 CHORALE

Chris M. Bernotas (ASCAP)

250 ORCHESTRAL REPERTOIRE: Symphony No. 45 "Farewell Symphony"

Franz Joseph Haydn (1732–1809)
Arranged by Jim Palmer (ASCAP)

Allegro assai

Concert A♭ Major

251 CONCERT A♭ MAJOR SCALE AND ARPEGGIO

252 CHROMATIC SCALE

253 BALANCE AND INTONATION: DIATONIC HARMONY

254 ORCHESTRAL REPERTOIRE: Symphony No. 1

Sir Edward Elgar (1857–1934)
Arranged by Jim Palmer (ASCAP)

Concert F Minor

255 CONCERT F MINOR SCALE AND ARPEGGIO

256 BALANCE AND INTONATION: DIATONIC HARMONY

257 ORCHESTRAL REPERTOIRE: Egmont Overture

Ludwig van Beethoven (1770–1827)
Arranged by Jim Palmer (ASCAP)

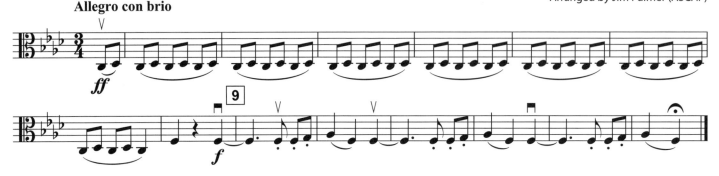

Concert E Major

258 **CONCERT E MAJOR SCALE AND ARPEGGIO**

259 **CHROMATIC SCALE**

260 **BALANCE AND INTONATION: DIATONIC HARMONY**

261 **ORCHESTRAL REPERTOIRE: Morning Mood from *Peer Gynt Suite No. 1***

Edvard Grieg (1843–1907)
Arranged by Jim Palmer (ASCAP)

Allegretto pastorale

Concert C♯ Minor

262 **CONCERT C♯ MINOR SCALE AND ARPEGGIO**

263 **BALANCE AND INTONATION: DIATONIC HARMONY**

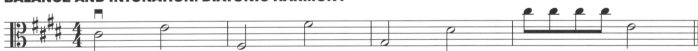

264 **ORCHESTRAL REPERTOIRE: Trauermarsch from *Symphony No. 5***

Gustav Mahler (1860–1911)
Arranged by Jim Palmer (ASCAP)

Etwas gehaltener

* A double sharp (✗) raises the pitch of a note two *half steps* or one *whole step*.

Modulation

265 **MODULATION: PARALLEL MAJOR TO MINOR**   Chris M. Bernotas (ASCAP)

266 **MODULATION: PARALLEL MAJOR TO MINOR**   Chris M. Bernotas (ASCAP)

267 **MODULATION: COMMON CHORD**   Chris M. Bernotas (ASCAP)

268 **MODULATION: COMMON CHORD**   Chris M. Bernotas (ASCAP)

269 **MODULATION: COMMON TONE**   Chris M. Bernotas (ASCAP)

270 **MODULATION: DIRECT**   Chris M. Bernotas (ASCAP)